WRESTLING BASICS

by **Ron Fox**

Illustrated by
Robert Schoolcraft

with Photographs

Created and Produced by
Arvid Knudsen

PRENTICE-HALL, Inc.

Englewood Cliffs, New Jersey

Dedication

This book is dedicated to a wonderful
family, the cornerstone of a very pleasant life.

Acknowledgments

Special thanks are given to several
people who helped in the formulation of
this book: Bruce Baumgartner, Chris
Catalfo, Bill Hyman, Dave McMahon,
Steve LePage, Gene Mills, Bill Savage.

Other **Sports Basics Books** in Series

BASKETBALL BASICS by Greggory Morris
RUNNING BASICS by Carol Lea Benjamin
DISCO BASICS by Maxine Polley
GYMNASTICS BASICS by John and Mary Jean Traetta
RACQUETBALL BASICS by Tony Boccaccio
FRISBEE DISC BASICS by Dan Roddick
SWIMMING BASICS by Rob Orr and Jane B. Tyler
HORSEBACK RIDING BASICS by Dianne Reimer
SKIING BASICS by Al Morrozzi
BASEBALL BASICS by Jack Lang
FISHING BASICS by John Randolph
FOOTBALL BASICS by Larry Fox
SOCCER BASICS by Alex Yannis
SAILING BASICS by Lorna Slocombe

BICYCLING BASICS by Tim and Glenda Wilhelm
BACKPACKING BASICS by John Randolph
TENNIS BASICS by Robert J. LaMarche
TRACK & FIELD BASICS by Fred McMane
HOCKEY BASICS by Norman MacLean
BOWLING BASICS by Chuck Pezzano
KARATE BASICS by Thomas J. Nardi
ICE-SKATING BASICS by Norman MacLean
WATERSPORTS BASICS by Don Wallace
CAMPING BASICS by Wayne Armstrong
BOATING BASICS by Henry F. Halsted
GOLF BASICS by Roger Schiffman
DIVING BASICS by Bob Goldberg

Text copyright © 1986 by Ron Fox and Arvid
Knudsen
Illustrations copyright © 1986 by Arvid Knudsen

Printed in the United States of America   · J

Prentice-Hall International (UK) Limited, London
Prentice-Hall of Australia, Pty. Ltd., Sydney
Prentice-Hall of Canada, Inc., Toronto
Prentice-Hall Hispanoamericana, S.A., Mexico
Prentice-Hall of India Private Ltd., New Delhi
Prentice-Hall of Japan, Inc., Tokyo
Prentice-Hall of Southeast Asia Pte. Ltd., Singapore
Whitehall Books Limited, Wellington, New Zealand
Editora Prentice-Hall do Brasil Ltda., Rio de Janeiro

10 9 8 7 6 5 4 3 2

Library of Congress Cataloging in Publication Data

Fox, Ron.
  Wrestling basics.

  Summary: Examines the history, basic positions,
rules, and scoring of wrestling.
    1. Wrestling—Juvenile literature. [1. Wrestling]
I. Schoolcraft, Robert, ill. II. Knudsen, Arvid.
III. Title.
GV1195.F68   1986   796.8'12   85-25595
ISBN 0-13-969320-3

CONTENTS

PHOTO CREDITS: P. 4, Courtesy of Gene Mills.
Pp. 5 and 13, Courtesy of *The Record.* Pp. 18, 24,
27, 28, 33, 34, 36, 37 and 38 Courtesy of
Stan Woods, Emerson High School, N.J.

4

BRUCE BAUMGARTNER,
1984 OLYMPIC HEAVYWEIGHT
CHAMPION.

1/ Introduction to Wrestling

There are many factors that make the sport of high school wrestling unique. Wrestling offers a blend of challenge and equality, opportunity and sacrifice. While it is a team sport, it spotlights the individual more than most other sports.

To engage in the sport takes a willingness to accept a challenge. And those who have accepted that challenge say they would not trade that opportunity for anything. The lessons learned in wrestling carry them through life.

Bruce Baumgartner, the 1984 Olympic heavyweight champion, compares wrestling to a fight with your brother. He terms it a rough individual sport, where you can release your tensions and frustrations. Wrestling is a physical sport, but it is closely monitored by referees who make sure the physical aspect does not get out of hand.

Is wrestling fun? Well, it is not exactly an activity that can be compared with kite flying. There is no continuous joy, because wrestling is hard work. But wrestlers who play other sports say there is no feeling in sports greater than an important victory in wrestling because it is one athlete against another, and the victory belongs only to one person—the athlete, who is completely responsible for the outcome. No sports accomplishment beats the great feeling of accomplishment derived from a wrestling win, say those who have experienced it.

GENE MILLS, FORMER NATIONAL COLLEGIATE
CHAMPION WHILE AT SYRACUSE UNIVERSITY, IS NOW
ASSISTANT WRESTLING COACH OF HIS ALMA MATER.

The camaraderie in wrestling is something special because it is fostered by the togetherness of athletes working hard together to be the best. They have shared the rigors of training, which is a special bond between them. Nearly 10,000 high schools throughout the nation have wrestling programs. The sport vies with basketball for popularity in the winter season, and in many towns in all areas of the United States, wrestling exceeds basketball in popularity.

But there's much more.

Although it is an individual sport, wrestling also has a team concept. Wrestling is an individual sport because you do well or make the mistakes yourself. When you are out on the mat, you cannot rely on your teammates to carry you. In a sport like football, one player's mistake can be covered up by his 11 teammates. That is not the case in wrestling.

There is less of an opportunity to make excuses in wrestling for that same reason. The only person who can be truly blamed for an individual loss is the individual wrestler.

Balance and opportunity are major parts of wrestling's makeup. Bouts are broken down by weight class, so size is no handicap, the way it can be in other sports. Wrestling is a sport made for a wider range of young people.

Although a 98-pounder is discouraged from trying out for football or basketball, and is told that his legs may be too short to allow him to run track successfully against long-legged opponents, he receives the opportunity in wrestling to become just as big a hero in school as any 220-pound linebacker.

Wrestling has a place for the 98-pounder, and it can be in a starring role. He needn't be a bench warmer or water boy because there is no such thing as a size handicap.

Gene Mills was a little 88-pounder as a 14-year-old high school freshman when he gave wrestling a try. Mills went on to All-American status, which he attained twice at Syracuse University, where he now coaches. He was a Pan American Games champion at 114.5 pounds in 1979, NCAA champion at 118 pounds in 1981, and went on to earn a position on the U.S. Olympic team in 1984.

Mills, who began referring to himself as "Mean Gene the Pinning Machine" late in his college career, claims he owes his self-esteem to wrestling. He says that while some people have difficulty dealing with difficult moments in life, he believes he can handle any of life's pitfalls because wrestling made him mentally tougher.

Wrestling also made Mills more organized, because in wrestling you must set goals and arrange your priorities.

Another positive factor is that wrestling is so balanced.

In basketball, a 6-foot-10 center who is guarded by a 6-foot-3 defender of comparable talent is likely to score more points than his shorter opponent because of the height factor. But such mismatches do not occur in wrestling.

Lineups in wrestling are much more fairly matched than in other sports. Lineups are dictated by predetermined weight classes, beginning with the lowest weights. In high school, the opening bout is limited to 98 pounds and below at the beginning of the season. Each weight class is allowed a small weight allowance later in the season, so the 98-pound classification eventually becomes the 101-pound class, and so on.

The bouts then are for increased weights, moving up through heavyweight (185 pounds and above). In high school, the weights are 101, 108, 115, 122, 129, 135, 141, 148, 158, 170, 188, and heavyweight. In college, they are 118, 126, 134, 142, 150, 158, 167, 177, 190, and heavyweight.

International weight classes are 114.5, 125.5, 138.5, 154, 171.5, 191.5, 213.5, and heavyweight.

The only imbalance occurs at heavyweight, where the super-heavy wrestler has a huge weight advantage against the 185-pounder who barely qualifies to wrestle in that weight class. High school wrestling has reduced that imbalance by mandating a limit of 275 pounds for heavyweights.

Weight classes are strictly controlled by the men who monitor the pre-meet scales. No wrestler may compete in a weight class if he weighs more than that class's limit. For instance, if a candidate for the 135-pound bout registers 136 pounds during the pre-meet weigh-in, he is required to either move up to a higher weight class or not to wrestle at all.

Thus, wrestling's goals of balance and fair play are maintained.

8 THE REFEREE'S WHISTLE HAS JUST SOUNDED THE
BEGINNING OF THE BOUT AND THE WRESTLERS,
STARTING ON THEIR FEET, GO ON TO THE ATTACK.

2 / A Short History of Wrestling

Wrestling was the logical beginning of sports, since it was a no-frills activity, totally basic: no ball was used, no net, no bat, no shinguards. It remains a sport that epitomizes the stripped-down version of the fight for survival: man against man—each seeking to overcome, control, and ultimately defeat the other.

Two weaponless men interested in one-on-one athletic competition, particularly two aggressive cavemen, were limited to forms of boxing or wrestling. Since it is difficult to picture two cavemen dancing and jabbing the way boxers do today, wrestling must be the oldest form of sports.

That fact is substantiated in many ways, beginning with cave drawings found in France and authenticated as being nearly 20,000 years old. The writings of Homer, the Greek poet, often describe athletic competitions. The most vivid is found in his classic tale, *The Iliad*, in which Odysseus and Ajax vie in a titanic match. According to another poet, Pindar, Zeus won claim to the entire universe when he outwrestled Cronus in 776 B.C., a victory that inspired the first Olympic Games.

Perhaps the finest work on the subject is *A Pictorial History of Wrestling*, by Graeme Kent, which points out that drawings (220 in all) on the Beni-Hasan tomb walls in Middle Egypt date back to 3400 B.C. They clearly show two figures involved in a series of wrestling moves, including some of today's prime moves, such as single-leg takedowns, headlocks, and Navy rides.

9

Evidence of serious wrestling dates back to 3015 B.C. in Israel, 2600 B.C. in Babylonia, and 1000 B.C. in China.

Roman Emperor Augustus is credited with starting a series of athletic festivals that included the Pythian Games and Nemean Games around A.D. 14. His encouragement gave birth to professional wrestling, as athletes traveled from festival to festival to win the prize money.

Wrestling officially became an Olympic sport during the eighteenth Olympiad in 708 B.C. It was an integral part of the program, which consisted originally of only five sports. Wrestling was last on the agenda, often the decisive event of the series.

The first intercollegiate wrestling match in the United States took place at the turn of the twentieth century, Yale versus the University of Pennsylvania.

In the past, hosting wrestling tournaments was a way to bring countries together. That remains the case today, since wrestling is one of the few areas in which the United States and Russia are of a single mind. Each believes in the importance of wrestling in society. The two superpowers continually send teams against each other for exhibition matches on either side of the Atlantic Ocean.

Among the most prolific of history's wrestlers have been Milo (540 B.C.) and Hercules (5 B.C.) of Greece, Roman Emperor Commodus (A.D. 180–193), and four twentieth-century stars Wakanohana of Japan, Georges Hackenschmidt of Russia, Tromp Van Diggelen of South Africa, and Dan Gable of the United States (who starred for the University of Iowa, where he later became head coach, as well as coach of the U.S. Olympic team).

What follows is a brief and basic introduction to what lies ahead for the young athlete contemplating a future in wrestling. But first, let's take a look at a breakdown of the various styles and related wrestling sports.

3 / Worldwide Wrestling Has Many Styles

Freestyle

The initial form of this wrestling style was usually referred to as "catch as catch can" and was the simplest, no-holds-barred form of today's freestyle method of wrestling.

The original form has been modified a bit. A wrestler may no longer kick or choke or slam his opponent to the mat. Gouging, kneeing, and hair-pulling are also not permitted. No hold or throw is allowed that is doled out for punishment alone.

Once a wrestler has taken down his opponent and has gained full control of him on the mat, freestyle officials allow him a few moments to attempt to turn his man. If the officials then believe he will not be able to turn his man quickly, they interrupt the proceedings and return the two wrestlers to their feet. In high school, however, the two wrestlers continue battling after the takedown.

Greco–Roman

In the early nineteenth century, the French were credited with devising what is now the Greco–Roman style. Yet there is evidence that the style emanated much earlier, around the year 186 B.C. The Etruscans had migrated from Asia Minor to Rome, where their style of wrestling attracted the attention of the Romans. And once the Romans conquered the Greeks, they added the nuances of several cultures, forming a mixture of styles.

One major weapon—tripping—is forbidden in Greco-Roman wrestling. In fact, rules revised over the years prohibit wrestlers from using their legs as weapons or from applying holds below the waist of their opponents.

The Greco-Roman style was added to the Olympics in 1896 and has grown in popularity ever since. Superior upper-body strength and balance are needed by a wrestler limited by the Greco-Roman rules.

High school and college wrestlers have learned that it is important to become familiar with the Greco-Roman style at an early point in their careers because it makes them more versatile on their feet, gives them a greater arsenal of takedown moves, and provides them with an advantage over the wrestler who relies only on the takedown basics of freestyle wrestling.

Although Chris Catalfo was a New Jersey High School champion and went on to attain All-American stature at Syracuse University, he did not try the Greco-Roman style until his college eligibility was over. And when he finally did turn to it, he had phenomenal success. In the space of nine months of hard work, he became so proficient in his new style that he made the U.S. Olympic wrestling team as a Greco-Roman specialist, thanks to the intense coaching of Albany (N.Y.) State College's Joe Demeo, the acknowledged expert in the field.

The moves, the philosophy, and the practices are all different in Greco-Roman. Yet, the ease with which Catalfo took to the Greco-Roman style amazed him as much as it amazed anyone else. In a freestyle tournament following the Olympics, he won an international tournament championship in Canada by defeating the then third-ranked 135-pounder in the world. Catalfo managed that feat in an unusual manner, using upper body holds.

Sombo

Hardly a household name, sombo wrestling has not gained as large a foothold in the world as wrestling's other major forms because it is not yet an Olympic sport. Sombo, also known in some countries as Sambo, is a combination of wrestling and judo that was popularized in Russia.

FORMER OLYMPIC WRESTLER CHRIS CATALFO IS
ATTEMPTING TO TURN — OR SWITCH — OUT OF THE
REFEREE'S POSITION.

Sumo

The Japanese specialty is for the big boys only. Sumo wrestlers usually weigh in, in the neighborhood of 300 pounds and are
regarded by the Japanese as national heroes. During their bout, following a lengthy ceremony, the combatants push against each other
like two massive rams with their horns locked, refusing to yield. The
object is to push the opponent out of the ring or down to the mat.
When either is accomplished, the bout is over.

Professional

Practitioners of all these forms of wrestling are quick to emphasize that professional wrestling is entirely different. The pro style is more theatrical than sporting and, while its wrestlers will deny that there is anything fishy about the proceedings, there are strong suspicions that all moves and the eventual outcome of each bout are predetermined and choreographed. Yet professional wrestling, with its exaggerated grunts and groans and methods—such as the choke hold, full nelson, and slam—that are outlawed in amateur wrestling, is hugely successful at the gate.

Professional Freestyle

Many of the nation's best collegiate wrestlers have found themselves at a crossroads in life with the advent of professional freestyle wrestling. Leagues were formed in 1984, and turning pro seemed to be the next logical step out of college, like an All-American football player being drafted by a National Football League team and then signing a hefty bonus contract.

But the question of whether such a new endeavor would survive served as a caution. Numerous college stars were reluctant to commit themselves. Once they signed professional contracts, there would be no turning back, they realized, because they no longer would be eligible to wrestle in amateur events, which include the Olympic Games and the World University Games.

The thought of Olympic competition continues to burn brightly in the minds and hearts of enough wrestlers, regardless of their age and the length of time between Olympic years. That is why signing a pro contract was such a difficult decision for them.

4 / Basic Rules of the Wrestling Bout

The arena is the high school or college gym, and the bout takes place on a foam-core plastic mat that is two inches thick. Wrestling takes place on that mat inside a circle 23 feet in diameter. Each wrestler wears a singlet—a one-piece stretch uniform—and must wear headgear.

In high school, the bout consists of three two-minute periods. In college, it is 2–3–3.

Most regular-season high school and college bouts are officiated by no more than one referee. Often in major tournaments, one or two mat judges are added as overseers who can overrule the referee's decisions or be ready to confer with him on other problems.

There is no rest between periods, but injury timeouts are granted. Often each wrestler is handed a thin strip of material in the form of an anklet to wear during the bout—one wearing green or blue, the other red—for scoring purposes.

The wrestlers start off on their feet, facing each other. In high school, a flip of a colored disc determines which wrestler will have a choice at the beginning of the second period. He may choose to start it in the same neutral standing position as in the first period, or he may select either the top or bottom in the *referee's position*.

The referee's position begins with the bottom man on all fours. The top man must have one hand on the adjacent arm of his opponent, while also wrapping the other arm around him.

THE MAT

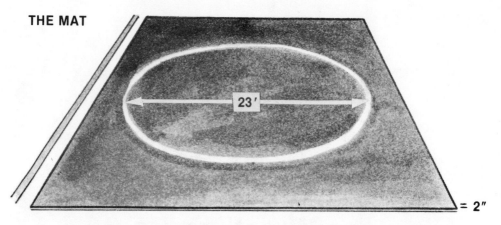

23'

= 2"

Wrestlers are proud to note that their sport is the true test of the warrior. Even though team scores are kept through points earned by the individuals, when it comes down to the bout itself, it is one-on-one—one wrestler against another. No teammate may intercede or have any effect on the bout. It is up to the wrestler to execute his moves on his own. A coach may shout instructions from the edge of the mat, but he cannot confer with his wrestler. There are no time-outs, although some coaches and wrestlers bend the rules by using feigned injuries to receive injury timeouts.

A victory by *pinning* your opponent to the mat is worth six team points. You are awarded a *pin* if you press your opponent's two shoulders or scapula to the mat and hold them there for five seconds.

The goal in wrestling is to pin, but there are other ways to win. Five points may be earned if a bout is decided by 12 or more points (superior decision) and four may be won if the bout is decided by from 8 to 11 points (major decision). Decisions with tighter margins earn three team points. If wrestlers fight to a tie during a regular dual-meet (two-team) bout, the result is called a draw and two points are awarded to each team.

The bout begins with both wrestlers on their feet, facing each other in the center of the mat. The referee begins the bout by blow-ing his whistle. Each wrestler is expected to *take down* the other, to bring the opponent down to the mat. There are many legal ways of taking down an opponent, including tripping, throwing, or merely

THE STANCE

knocking him off balance. Two points are awarded for the take-down, but the wrestler must be fully in charge of his opponent in order to gain takedown points.

If the opponent still has a substantial grip on the top man's leg, arm, or head, the takedown will not be called by the official.

The referee watches to make sure that the top man continues to wrestle aggressively. The top man must strive to pin his opponent or he will be warned for *stalling*. The bottom man, meanwhile, must not be allowed to roll up in a ball as a part of his defense. He, too, must be aggressive and work not only to fend off the pin attempt, but also to improve his position.

The referee also is conscious of holds that can cause serious injury. He will frequently stop bouts and signal by placing his right hand behind his neck—a sign that it was a hold he considered potentially dangerous. He is there not only to rule for or against the wrestlers, but also to protect them.

WRESTLER ON RIGHT "RIDES" HIS MAN, WHILE HIS OPPONENT ATTEMPTS TO RISE FROM THE REFEREE'S POSITION.

THE TWO WRESTLERS THRUST AND PARRY, SEEKING A TAKEDOWN.

5 / The Attack

Takedowns

You have recorded a takedown when you have forced your opponent down from a standing position onto the mat and have taken control of him. The takedown is worth a score of two points.

It would seem that when two people do battle, the stronger battler will prevail. But that is not necessarily so. While brute strength may be a factor in some sports, it is not necessarily a successful wrestler's most important attribute.

Conditioning, balance, leverage, and craftiness are your best weapons if used singly or together. They are just as important and, at times, even more important than strength alone.

Catching an opponent off balance often is a key to a less muscular wrestler's defeating a more powerful wrestler in a match. Rather than becoming a victim of a stronger wrestler's assault, his opponent often can benefit by "going with the flow," allowing the stronger wrestler to be placed in jeopardy by his own momentum.

A valuable statement for wrestlers young and old to remember is that the wrestler who records the opening takedown does more than merely put his opponent to the mat. The takedown provides an exhilarating feeling, gains momentum and confidence while lessening the opponent's confidence, and often is described by winning wrestlers as the key to their entire repertoire.

Following are a few of the basic takedowns.

Single-, Double-Leg

The basic takedown begins with a deep step forward and a lunge at an opponent's feet, called *shooting*. Catching a single leg or both legs and knowing what to do once you have latched onto a limb or limbs is a prime bit of wrestling know-how. Catching a leg and lifting it as high as possible obviously puts the opponent in a desperate position. The double-leg is more of a tackle. Once the two legs are encased by the arms of the attacking wrestler, he may go in one or two directions: lifting and dumping the opponent or switching off to a single-leg pickup.

DOUBLE LEG TAKEDOWN

The Duck Under

Wrestler A, appearing to concentrate on an upper-body move, suddenly ducks his head to the side of Wrestler B and steps around him, bringing him down from behind.

DUCK UNDER

21

The Hip Roll

Also known as the *whizzer*, the hip roll's popularity has increased dramatically over the past decade. Glamour may be part of the reason, since the hip roll is more flamboyant than most takedown moves and resembles a judo move. In fact, many wrestlers with judo or karate backgrounds consider the hip roll their No. 1 weapon because it is so closely related to the moves they are used to performing. In this case, familiarity breeds more comfort and confidence.

A wrestler who has locked up his opponent by tying his arms up high has set up the whizzer. He crosses a leg in front of his opponent while turning slightly, digging a hip into the opponent's midsection or upper thigh. Then, with a yank, he pulls with an arm while he pushes in with the hip, rolling his opponent over and onto the mat, preferably putting him to his back and in immediate jeopardy.

The move can be good for as many as five points—two for the takedown plus two or three for back points.

HIP ROLL

The Headlock

Simply put, a wrestler overpowers his opponent by wrapping an arm around the opponent's head and squeezing, either forcing the man straight down or throwing him with a combination that includes the whizzer's hip roll.

HEADLOCK

1

2

3

4

BEARHUG

Bearhug

The bearhug is a favorite of bigger, stronger, bearlike wrestlers who attack the upper body, locking the opponent in a viselike grip and either throwing him sideways to the mat or simply caving him in by charging against the upper body, driving him backward.

1

2

23

SOME MOVES ARE SPECTACULAR. HERE THE BOY IN DANGER OF BEING PINNED HAS BEEN THROWN ON TO HIS BACK WITH AN ARMLOCK.

A Varied Attack

It is foolhardy to attempt to master too many takedown moves because such a plan may leave a wrestler with no move he can truly depend upon. He would be like the man who is a jack of all trades but the master of none. It is better to perfect one move before adopting a second takedown method of attack.

Yet it is best for the wrestler to take the time to perfect more than one sure thing for his takedown arsenal.

For example, a wrestler who has had phenomenal success with a single-leg takedown may find the move ineffective on a higher level of wrestling; for instance, the high school districts, regionals, or state finals. More efficient wrestlers may possess countermoves that can shut off a certain takedown move, especially if the move is all the other wrestler has to offer.

It is then that the seemingly invincible takedown artist is left unusually ineffective. It is a terribly helpless feeling and makes the wrestler wish he had learned another takedown.

6 / The Defense

Counters

Wrestling is a game of constant learning, and the rookie learns quickly that there is a counter for every move yet devised. For instance, the single-leg shoot can be countered by sprawling the legs backward, out of reach, while using the arms to press down on the head and shoulders of the attacking wrestler. The duck under is foiled if the defending wrestler can catch the head or arm of the attacker and turn it to his advantage.

The hip roll is countered by a similar thrust, causing the battling opponents to appear more like a wrestler facing a mirror. The defender, in fighting off the hip roll, locks in the same type of hold and tries to throw his man with a hip roll of his own. Instead of being pulled over his opponent and onto the mat, the defender applies the brakes by hipping into his opponent and turns the action the other way, attempting to pull over his attacker. The effort usually results in a stalemate.

There are hundreds of moves in wrestling and for each there is a counter. The more experience you have, the more natural it becomes to counter your opponent's moves.

1

2

3

Composure

It is interesting to watch the way a wrestler reacts to being taken down by his opponent. Again, experience plays a major role in handling the situation.

As the experienced wrestler realizes that his counters have failed and that he is headed inevitably for the mat, he still can throw a monkey wrench into his opponent's plans. He does not wait until he has hit the mat to launch his next wave of defense. In midflight, he concedes the takedown but vows to limit his opponent to two points.

The falling warrior shifts his body on the way down, making sure to land on either his stomach or his side, thus preventing his opponent from adding immediate back points.

Again, it is a reaction bred by hours of practice and months of actual wrestling.

THE WHITE-UNIFORMED WRESTLER AVOIDS BEING
TAKEN COMPLETELY DOWN BY BRACING HIMSELF WITH
HIS HANDS AND ARMS.

TOP WRESTLER USES A TWO-ON-ONE RIDE, TWO HANDS
CLAMPING DOWN ON ONE WRIST.

7 / Riding Grips, Reversals, Escapes, and Pinning

Riding Grips

There are numerous holds available to the top wrestler who wishes to remain in command. One of the most popular rides is the *two-on-one*, in which the man in control wraps his arms around his opponent from the rear and uses both hands to grip one of the bottom man's arms. The hold helps keep the bottom man from bracing himself upward with his arms. The key to maintaining command is breaking down the ''base'' of the opponent.

It is not enough merely to control an opponent. The top wrestler must work on pinning combinations or be flagged for *stalling*. Continuous action is demanded by the referee. A second stalling call results in one point being awarded to the nonstaller's team, as does a third call. A fourth stalling call brings two points, and a fifth encourages the referee to call a default loss against the stalling wrestler.

TWO-ON-ONE RIDE

1   2   3

HALF NELSON

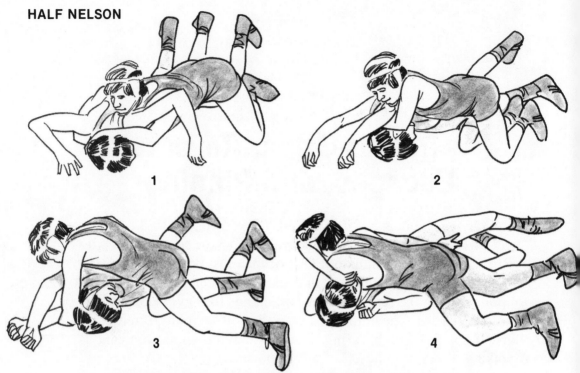

1

2

3

4

The default loss is most costly to a team, since the opposition is awarded six team points, the equivalent to a win by pin.

Other riding grips that are popular today include the *half nelson*, the *arm bar*, the *Navy ride*, and the *stack*. The latter two consist of using the opponent's legs to steer him to his back. The half nelson and arm bar are particularly effective at forcing the man over and onto his back.

The start of the ride becomes as important as the takedown at the beginning of the bout. The quickest move out of the referee's position can turn the momentum of a bout. The top man is told that it is imperative to get the jump and destroy the bottom man's initial move before it can get underway. The bottom man knows he has to make his first move count against a strong rider or he'll be cemented permanently to the mat. Yet, caution is important, because an over-anticipating wrestler who jumps the gun and moves before the referee's whistle sounds will be hit with a warning. One more such infraction and his opponent receives a penalty point.

Reversals

Simply put, the bottom man gains a reversal and two points once he turns the tables and becomes the top man.

If he cannot achieve the reversal, there remain two ways for the bottom man to score one point: (1) If he works his way to a position in which neither wrestler holds a physical advantage—neither controls the other—he is rewarded with one point for a neutral position; and (2) If, instead, the bottom man breaks free, he receives a point for an escape, and the standing thrust and parry portion of the bout resumes.

Types of reversals most popular include the *switch*, which is a quick turn that can be attempted from a sitting, standing, or kneeling position; the *headlock*; the *standup*; and a series of *rolls*.

OUTSIDE SWITCH

1 2

3 4 5

31

Escapes

Getting up off the bottom is no simple task for a wrestler going against another man of comparable size. Often it is tedious work, done step by step, getting back up to a kneeling position while the top man attempts to break down such bases by cutting the arms out from under the bottom man.

Once back to a sitting or kneeling position, the battle is at least half won. Then, other maneuvers may be put into play, such as *switches* or another crowd pleaser, the *run-and-tear*. In the latter maneuver, the bottom man gets up to his feet and tries to pry apart his opponent's hands while attempting to run away from his tormentor. The battle becomes a chase, and the top man suddenly becomes more of a tackler than a wrestler.

Pinning

The bout is over if a wrestler falls victim to a pin, also called a *fall*. A wrestler is pinned if both his shoulders or scapula are held to the mat for two seconds. If a wrestler is brought close enough to the mat, his opponent can gain either two or three *predicament*, or *near-fall*, points. One shoulder must be on the mat and the other must be within 45 degrees of the mat for the points to be awarded. It is a three-point reward if the predicament lasts five seconds or longer and a two-point reward if it lasts less than five seconds.

The half nelson, headlock, and arm bar—or bar arm—are the three most popular moves in working pinning combinations, many of which result in a cradle pin.

In applying a *half nelson*, a wrestler slides an arm under his opponent's arm and weaves upward, locking it in behind the opponent's neck. The *headlock* is self-explanatory, except that an arm lock must accompany the head grip to be legal. The *arm bar* is begun by pulling the arm back across an opponent's back hard enough to force his body to follow, eventually pulling him to his back. The *cradle* usually is a combination headlock and leg lift, as the man in control lies perpendicular to his foe, rocking him backward.

WHITE-UNIFORMED WRESTLER STARTS A HALF NELSON.

THE REFEREE TAKES A CLOSE LOOK TO SEE IF THE
WRESTLER'S SHOULDER IS PRESSED TO THE MAT. IF SO,
IT IS A PIN.

8 / Other Factors

Criteria

One of the most confusing moments in wrestling occurs when two opponents have finished in a tie after three periods of a tournament bout and after three one-minute overtime periods. Then, a winner is decided by a list of criteria that is decided upon by the U.S. Wrestling Federation.

To its credit, USWF stays on top of its sport and remains willing to make changes in its rules if they are for the betterment of the sport. That attitude results in frequent changes in the order of criteria. Referees who try desperately to keep up with the many rules carefully consult the rule book following a tied bout, painstakingly going over the criteria step by step before awarding a decision victory to one of the wrestlers.

The No. 1 criterion generally concerns penalty points. The wrestler who receives the fewest penalty points for misconduct is declared the winner. Other criteria include the number of points earned for near-falls, the greater number of takedowns, reversals, escapes, stalling penalties, and the fewest stall warnings. If the tie remains after all the criteria have been applied, the officials award the victory to the wrestler who displays the most overall wrestling ability and aggressiveness.

THE AGGRESSIVE WRESTLER IN WHITE UNIFORM HOOKS
A LEG AND GOES FOR THE PIN.

Stamina

A strong finish becomes important in a tight bout. Many bouts that carry into the third and final period or into overtime are won by the better conditioned wrestler. Extra running, extra strenuous workouts in the wrestling room, and an extra careful allegiance to a proper diet pay off in difficult regular-season battles. Oddly, there are times when the apparently unbeatable wrestler finds himself in the most trouble when the bout reaches the third period, because he may be used to pinning in the first or second period and subconsciously has not built the stamina needed for the entire six-minute bout.

In the past, keeping an opponent underfoot was more important in high school wrestling than it is at present. A wrestler received an extra point when he *rode*—stayed atop—his opponent one minute longer than his opponent was able to hold the advantage. But, while that rule remains in effect in collegiate wrestling, it has been abolished at the high school level.

Members of the U.S. Wrestling Federation believed the riding time clock was one of the chief reasons for prolonged stalling. So they dropped riding time, further proof that the Federation is greatly concerned with providing a fast-moving, entertaining sport to watch.

THE FANS ARE KEPT INFORMED OF THE TIME REMAINING, THE PERIOD, BOUT SCORE, AND TEAM SCORE BY THE UPRIGHT ELECTRIC CLOCK AND TIMER.

Wrestling Etiquette

There is something special about wrestling in the way the athletes conduct themselves on the mat. Proper etiquette is drilled into each wrestler. No arguing with the referee is permitted. No disrespect may be exhibited, for fear of expulsion, which would result in a six-point default of the bout.

No headgear may be thrown, no tantrums are allowed. Somehow, the coaches make that point perfectly clear. Rarely is a wrestler found to be out of line, no matter how bad the call, no matter how painful the defeat. It is one of the wonders of sports.

SPORTSMANSHIP IS MANDATORY IN WRESTLING. THERE ARE SEVERAL MANDATORY HANDSHAKES.

Starting a Career

Wrestling is not for the easily discouraged. Dedication and commitment are two essentials. The majority of successful wrestlers will concede that they were not immediate successes. They will tell of terrible defeats that they suffered early in their careers. They also will emphasize one important fact that you should remember: they learned from every defeat. Losing badly seems to be as informative a lesson as any taught at a clinic or in a classroom. Bill Hyman, the 1985 NCAA heavyweight champion from Temple University had a meager 5–6 record as a varsity sophomore in high school. He worked to improve and was 18–5 as a junior. He kept running and lifting every day and won a New Jersey State championship as a senior and earned his college scholarship. By his junior year in college, Hyman was second in the nation among heavyweights, even though he weighed only 228 pounds.

He used to wrestle good people and lose, but if it was only by two points, he felt good. But then he decided that if he could be within two points of them, he could beat them. So he worked harder. You can't worry about what your opponent has done in the past. The main thing is to have a positive frame of mind. It works wonders.

Another mark of a good wrestler is a wardrobe filled with T-shirts from assorted summer camps. Good wrestlers quickly learn that there is more to their sport than reporting for duty in November and packing their gear in March. Summer camps and clinics are vital to their overall success, as are off-season schedules of weight lifting and running. It is all part of the regimen.

One new move picked up or one old one perfected can boost an athlete's regular-season record considerably.

While their friends may consider serious wrestlers insane for competing in summer tournaments in hot gyms instead of joining them on trips to a beach, they will wind up applauding those same wrestlers during the winter. The wrestler seems to thrive when he spends serious time on the sport and dedicates himself to personal sacrifice. Wrestling has to be a major part of your life if you want to be a champion.

One of those sacrifices is sticking to a careful diet. A wrestler's weight must remain steady. If he pigs out after a win, he must get back to work the following day and pare off whatever poundage he gained through his celebrating. While a basketball player can eat a pizza on the way to a game, his winter counterpart, the wrestler, cannot. A weigh-in at the site of the match is the first order of business. A celery stick or two is about all some wrestlers can handle during the hours before a weigh-in.

9/ The Importance of Experience

There is something addictive about wrestling that keeps athletes coming back for more, even after their primary goals have been achieved. Bill Hyman should have been satisfied with his NCAA championship, but he did not pack his bags and rest on his laurels. Only a few months later, Hyman was competing in an open tournament in Old Bridge, New Jersey. He loved the sport that much and remained immensely dedicated to it. He had to sign up for any tournament he could get to. There's something about wrestling that gets in your blood.

It is important for a wrestler to know that experience is just as important as strength or balance. An athlete better versed in the nuances of the sport is likely to be able to overcome certain deficiencies.

While learning, a wrestler is likely to be losing. But that is not to say that a losing wrestler cannot be a hero. If a badly beaten underdog wrestler manages to avoid being pinned, he does his team a great service by saving the team anywhere from one to three points.

Such a courageous effort can make the difference between a team's tie and loss, or a win and a tie. The effort can have an even greater impact on the overall match. It also may provide the impetus to victory—a psychological advantage, a momentum builder. The wind can be taken out of the other team's sails when its highly favored wrestler fails to record the pin that was considered a certainty. While at the other side of the mat, a team is inspired when one of its underdogs performs the unusual.

The Regimen

In many areas, there are wrestling programs run by private organizations, clubs, and Y's for anyone who is past 5 years of age. Attendance at Midget or Biddie programs often is a boon to a wrestler's career. But it is important that such programs serve as fun sessions, as an introduction to the sport, and not present a pressure-cooker atmosphere that can drive away a youngster. It is too early for a youngster to have to contend with the problem of making weight. Coaches at beginner levels should take that into consideration.

In many cases, especially in summer tournaments, there is great flexibility when it comes to matchups. There is no rigid weight rule. Instead of weight classes, there are weight groups where a youngster can weigh anywhere from 50 to 60 pounds in one group or from 61 to 70 pounds in the next group. There is no pressure to cut weight in order to wrestle.

The serious wrestler attends clinics and camps and enters himself in summer tournaments, to roll around on a mat with talented people from whom he can learn more. Weight lifting and running for stamina also are prime activities that add to his wrestling improvement.

The preparation begins during practices which are particularly draining. A team usually has set aside what is called the "wrestling room," either a room or a portion of the gym, where spirited practice is held for a few hours each day after school.

The work usually begins with the head coach and his assistants demonstrating a move or a hold. The athletes then pair off—for example, the two lightest in weight work together and on up the weight scale.

The number of actual bouts per season varies across the nation, but generally a team has two dual meets per week. A dual meet is a series of 12 bouts wrestled against another team. League standings are compiled, just as in any other high school and college sport. Following the regular high school season, many states have team tournaments to determine the best teams in the state.

After that comes the individual tournaments, the districts, the regions, and then the states. As the names suggest, the district tournament includes teams from nearby areas, from eight to 12

teams per district. The successful wrestlers move on to the regions, where they meet the top wrestlers from other nearby districts.

In some states, the district champions and runners-up advance to the regions, but other states also allow the third-place finishers to advance, too. The same is true for the final rounds of the states, in which the 1–2– or 1–2–3–place winners are eligible to move on.

Ask other wrestlers what makes their sport so special and the answers may draw you closer to signing up.

To many athletes, the highlight of wrestling is the opportunity to step out on a mat and determine their own success, without relying on another teammate.

Positives

To a man, wrestlers point to their sport as being an aid to their growth process. The sport aids them in becoming better organized, more disciplined, and more dependable, they say. They are better able to budget their time because of it.

Also, the wrestler who dedicates himself will be in excellent shape and will have no qualms about spending a day at the beach, because he has earned a physique that will be admired.

There is a great camaraderie developed in wrestling. It is as though all wrestlers are part of some large fraternity, as if going through the rigors of the sport, especially the difficult times faced early in a career, serve as a sort of initiation and make being a wrestler something very special.

Wrestling fans are loyal and fanatical and will follow a team everywhere.

Another factor in the closeness of the fraternity may be because of the greater popularity enjoyed by basketball in some areas. Where basketball reigns as the king of the winter, wrestlers may become more closeknit, feeling a stronger need to share their experiences and to rally together against the adversity of being unappreciated.

Negatives

A wrestler's one major drawback is the difficulty of maintaining a specific weight. Once a lineup is decided upon early in the season, it is hard for a wrestler to handle his normal growth. When a good wrestler adds a few pounds and tries to move up a weight class in the lineup, he may have to challenge for the starting berth. Most coaches allow what is called a wrestle-off at the end of a team practice session, as the candidate and the wrestler who holds the starting assignment in the coveted position vie for that position.

Some of the season's best bouts are not seen by the general public because they are waged behind closed doors, in a team's wrestling room, where the wrestle-off takes place.

Coaches are cautious about the ramifications of the wrestle-off because a team can be hurt if the two athletes are both talented wrestlers and the vacancy left by the ascending wrestler cannot be filled adequately. That is why some coaches discourage such movement, stressing that it can only result in a disrupted team lineup.

If the wrestle-off is allowed, the athlete who loses the wrestle-off then either drops down to the junior varsity or attempts to wrestle at another weight on the varsity level.

If a growing wrestler attempts to hold down his weight for the entire season—thus fighting his natural growth—he may be tempted to abuse himself by using diuretics to empty the system and thus cut a few pounds. Another abuse that has caused concern is a wrestler's decision to force himself to vomit. While the practice is strictly forbidden, there is always the fear that a coach with a win-or-else philosophy may not be so strictly opposed. The dangers of these practices should prevent the wrestler from using them.

A wrestler so caught up with the need to maintain his weight and not let down his team may force himself to lose fluids. He may do it without the approval of his coach. But such extreme measures can cause irreparable physical damage. Supervised exercise and balanced, sensible diets are the only way for intelligent wrestlers to contend with the ever present problem of maintaining weight.

Caution: There is enough pressure on a wrestler to perform to his peak, to work for his team as well as himself, and to maintain his weight. There is no need for a thoughtless parent to heap more pressure on the athlete. Too many parents attempt to relive their own successes or failures through their children, which can place undue pressure on them.

All your parents should expect is that you work hard and fulfill your commitment to the coach and the team. It is your responsibility to do your best for the whole season.

Young wrestlers—sixth- or seventh-graders—should also get involved in other sports. Youngsters who only wrestle can burn themselves out. It's got to be fun, too. Once you get to high school, you can specialize in wrestling—it's a great way to win a college scholarship.

Is the sport of wrestling really for you? It certainly is worth a tryout.

The start is pretty obvious. Contact the head wrestling coach at your local high school. Most wrestling coaches are deeply involved in the sport. They not only teach it, they are immersed in it. They know where the good camps are and when and where the best clinics are held. And they know where special areas for off-season practice will be set up.

It would not hurt to talk to a few accomplished wrestlers, who might be able to steer you toward the right off-season instructors. Wrestling is a closeknit sport, where advanced wrestlers usually are quite willing to teach what they know to newcomers.

A veteran wrestler can show you good habits to form and also can point out mistakes he made as a rookie wrestler that you may be able to avoid.

Also, call your local recreation director. More information on camps and clinics can be obtained there, too.

Further information about wrestling is available by writing to the National Federation of State High School Associations, 11724 Plaza Circle, Box 20626, Kansas City, MO 64195. Enclose your name and address and ask them to send information on high school wrestling.

Remember, wrestling is hard work. Gene Mills, the former Syracuse University All-American, became so involved in wrestling, he once wrote a poem about the sport:

This I say to be the best,
To be yourself and not like the rest.
Work real hard to be real tough,
But 100 percent is not good enough.
Set the impossible as being your goal,
Then reach deep inside from within your soul.
All you've got is all you could ask,
To help you achieve your impossible task.

Remember, too, not to become discouraged when success does not come to you immediately. Give the sport time. The world of wrestling is waiting for you. The challenge is there and, remember, there is as much fun involved as there is hard work. Good luck.

GLOSSARY

Arm bar. Top man holds forearm of opponent and presses with the upper part of other arm against back of his opponent's elbow or upper arm.

Arm drags. Maneuvers by which a wrestler grabs opponent's arm and pulls or posts it in order to go behind.

Bottom position. When a wrestler assumes a four-point stance at the start of a period or when a referee signals a restart, he is in the bottom position, the position of disadvantage.

Break down. Maneuver intended to knock out the opponent's supporting points and flatten him to the mat.

Bridge. A move in which the opponent about to be pinned braces his body on top of head, elbows, and feet to keep shoulders off the mat.

Control. One wrestler is positioned in such a way (behind and above his opponent) that his opponent is immobilized or restrained.

Counter. A maneuver in which one wrestler stops or reverses a maneuver by his opponent, to his advantage.

Cradle. A pinning maneuver in which one wrestler holds his opponent's head and leg in his arms and forces them toward each other, locking his hands.

Defensive position. Same as bottom position.

Double armlock. One wrestler locks his arm around his opponent's body from the front after reaching through his arms.

Double-leg takedown. One wrestler attacks his opponent's legs in an effort to take him to the mat.

Duck under. Maneuver in which one wrestler slips his head under his opponent's arm and uses his head as a fulcrum for leverage.

Escape. One wrestler frees himself from the control of the other.

Fall. A wrestler holds his man's shoulders or area of both scapulas to the mat for 1 second (in college), 2 seconds (in high school).

Finish-off. The final step in an offensive move that completes control of the opponent.

Forward roll. An escape or reverse in which one wrestler puts his shoulders to the mat and rolls rapidly and forcefully across them.

Full nelson. One opponent applies pressure against the back of his opponent's neck by reaching under his arms and locking his hands behind his neck. An illegal and dangerous hold.

Half nelson. One wrestler reaches under his opponent's arm from the rear and uses the back of his opponent's head or neck for leverage.

Inside crotch hold. One wrestler reaches between his opponent's legs and uses his forearm as a lever to prevent him from turning.

Mat. The soft padded material used as the wrestling arena.

Match. A competition between two wrestlers.

Near fall. A position in which the offensive wrestler has his opponent in a controlled pinning situation.

Nelson. A series of wrestling holds that features leverage applied under the armpit and behind the neck.

Neutral position. Both wrestlers face each other on their feet or on their knees with neither man in control.

Offensive position. Same as top position.

One-on-one. The offensive wrestler uses one hand to control one hand of the defensive wrestler.

Penalty points. Points awarded to one wrestler when his opponent violates a rule or procedure.

Penetration. One wrestler drives deep through his opponent's defenses.

Pin. See Fall.

Referee's position. Starting position for the opening of the second and third periods of a match and for all restarts not from a neutral position. Wrestlers take a top and bottom as directed by the referee.

Reversal. A 2-point scoring move that occurs when one wrestler frees himself of the control of his opponent and gains control.

Reverse nelson. One wrestler lifts against the back of his opponent's head by reaching under his arm from in front of him.

Riding time. The net amount of time one wrestler controls his opponent.

Roll. A series of maneuvers in which one wrestler rolls his opponent's weight, placing himself momentarily on his side and back or across his shoulders.

Scissors. One wrestler encircles his opponent's thigh with his legs and squeezes him by crossing his ankles.

Set-up. A maneuver by which one wrestler tries to gain a slight advantage by feinting, pulling, pushing, or making noises to distract his opponent.

Single-leg takedown. Any maneuver by which an attacking wrestler gains control of one of his opponent's legs to force him to the mat.

Stack. A pinning maneuver in which one wrestler lifts his opponent's hips and buttocks above his upper body.

Stalemate. A position other than a pinning situation in which neither wrestler can nor will improve his position.

Stalling. Failure to wrestle aggressively. Avoiding action.

Stand-up. A maneuver by which a wrestler on the bottom bursts to his feet.

Takedown. One wrestler takes his opponent to the mat from a neutral position.

Three-quarter nelson. One wrestler applies pressure to the back of his opponent's head or neck with two hands interlocked by reaching under only one arm and under the chest to the far side.

Throw. One wrestler knocks his opponent off his feet and aims his back toward the mat.

Top position. One wrestler is above and behind his opponent with one arm encircling his waist and another placed loosely on his elbow. Position of advantage.

Two-on-one hold. One wrestler grabs his opponent's arm or wrist with both hands.

Wrestler's grip. The interlocking of the two hands in order to apply the greatest pressure or lock possible.

INDEX

796.8   Fox, Ron
FO
        Wrestling basics

$10.95

DATE			
	1999		

A4064